Sasha's Sleepover

by Katie Dale

illustrated by Ashley King

Sasha and Jane were friends. Sasha liked Jane a lot. However, she couldn't help feeling slightly jealous.

Jane was clever, sporty and musical. She had amazing one-of-a-kind clothes.

"I have to go away for work tonight," Sasha's mum said after school. "You're staying with your cousins."

"Do I have to?" Sasha sighed. "The baby cries all night."

Her mum frowned.

"You're welcome to stay with us," Jane's mum, Lorraine, offered.

Sasha's face lit up. "Can I, Mum? Please?" she said. Sasha's mum agreed.

It was a long walk to Jane's flat. Sasha wondered why they didn't drive or catch the bus.

"We're halfway there," Jane said cheerfully.

"Only halfway?" Sasha gasped, puffing as they climbed a big hill.

"It's good exercise," Jane pointed out.

Jane's flat felt tiny to Sasha. It was roughly the same size as Sasha's lounge.

"Where's your TV?" Sasha asked, surprised.

"I borrow library books," Jane explained. "It's better for the planet. Who needs a TV when you have your imagination."

“Let’s make an igloo,” Jane grinned. She headed to the recycling pile.

“From rubbish?” Sasha said, surprised.

“One person’s rubbish is another person’s riches,” Jane giggled.

It was fun making the igloo. It even felt as cold as the Arctic. Sasha shivered and coughed.

"Would you like to borrow a jumper?" Jane offered.

"Yes, please," Sasha said.

Sasha gazed jealously at Jane's fabulous clothes. "Where do you get them all?" she asked.

"From me," Lorraine called. "I've got a new bag of charity shop rejects today."

Jane cheered, but Sasha was confused.

"Who'd want clothes rejected by a charity shop?" she wondered.

"This jacket's gorgeous – apart from the stains," Jane said. She touched the sleeves. "They'll be tough to get out."

"I could replace them with the sleeves from this?" Lorraine suggested. She held up a sequinned sweatshirt.

"That sounds great," Jane cried.

Sasha smiled. So that's why all Jane's clothes were one-of-a-kind. Lorraine made them. Lucky Jane!

"Would you like a jacket too, Sasha?" Lorraine offered generously. "It's no trouble."

Sasha nodded. "I'd love one!"

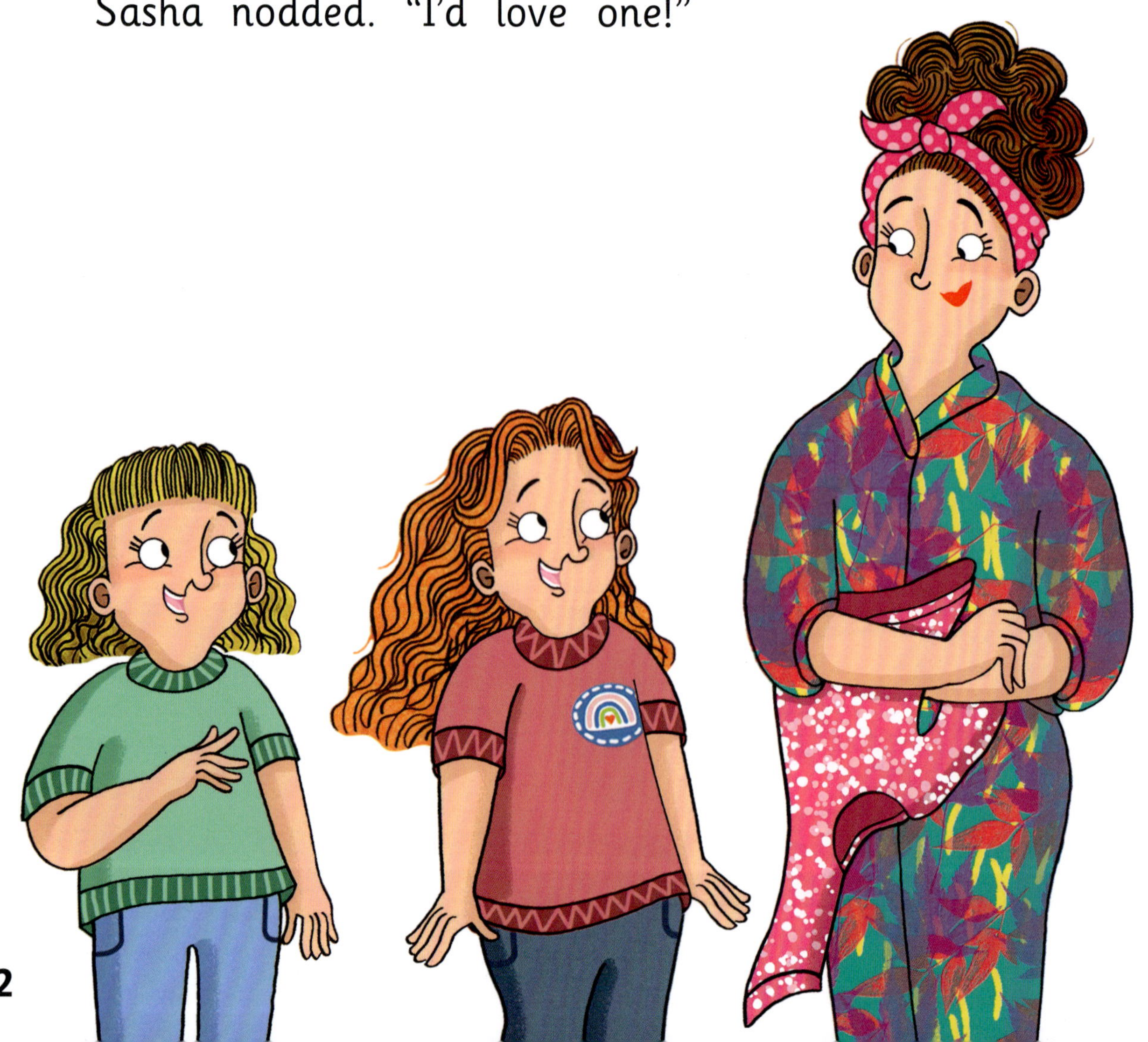

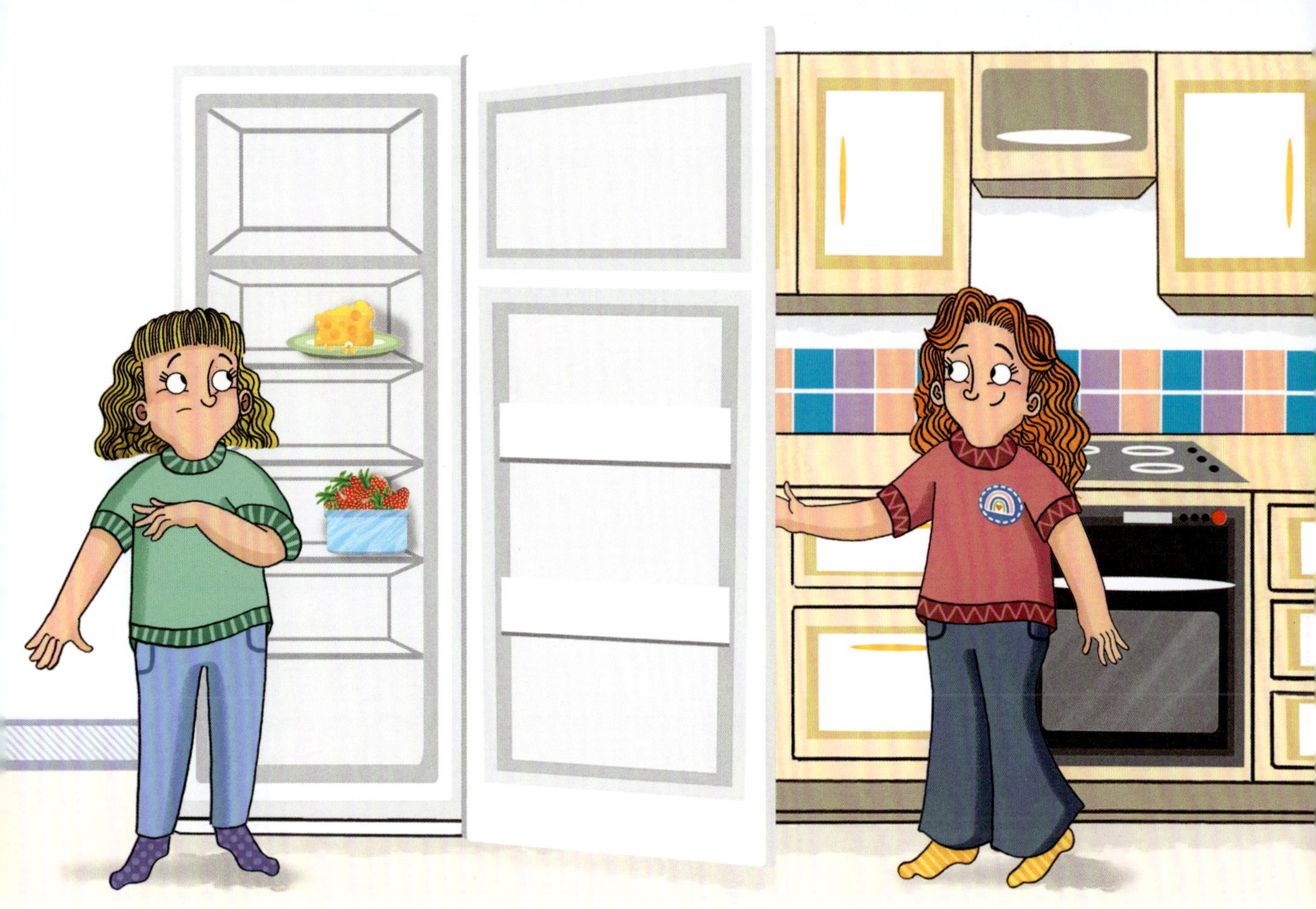

"Let's make dinner while Mum works," Jane said.

She opened the fridge. It was empty apart from a bit of cheese and some strawberries.

Sasha frowned. Had Lorraine forgotten to go shopping?

“Strawberries!” Jane cried delightedly. “Yum! What a treat.”

“Mrs Chang picked them from the communal garden,” Lorraine called. “She gave me a couple of potatoes, too.”

“Double yum!” Jane beamed.

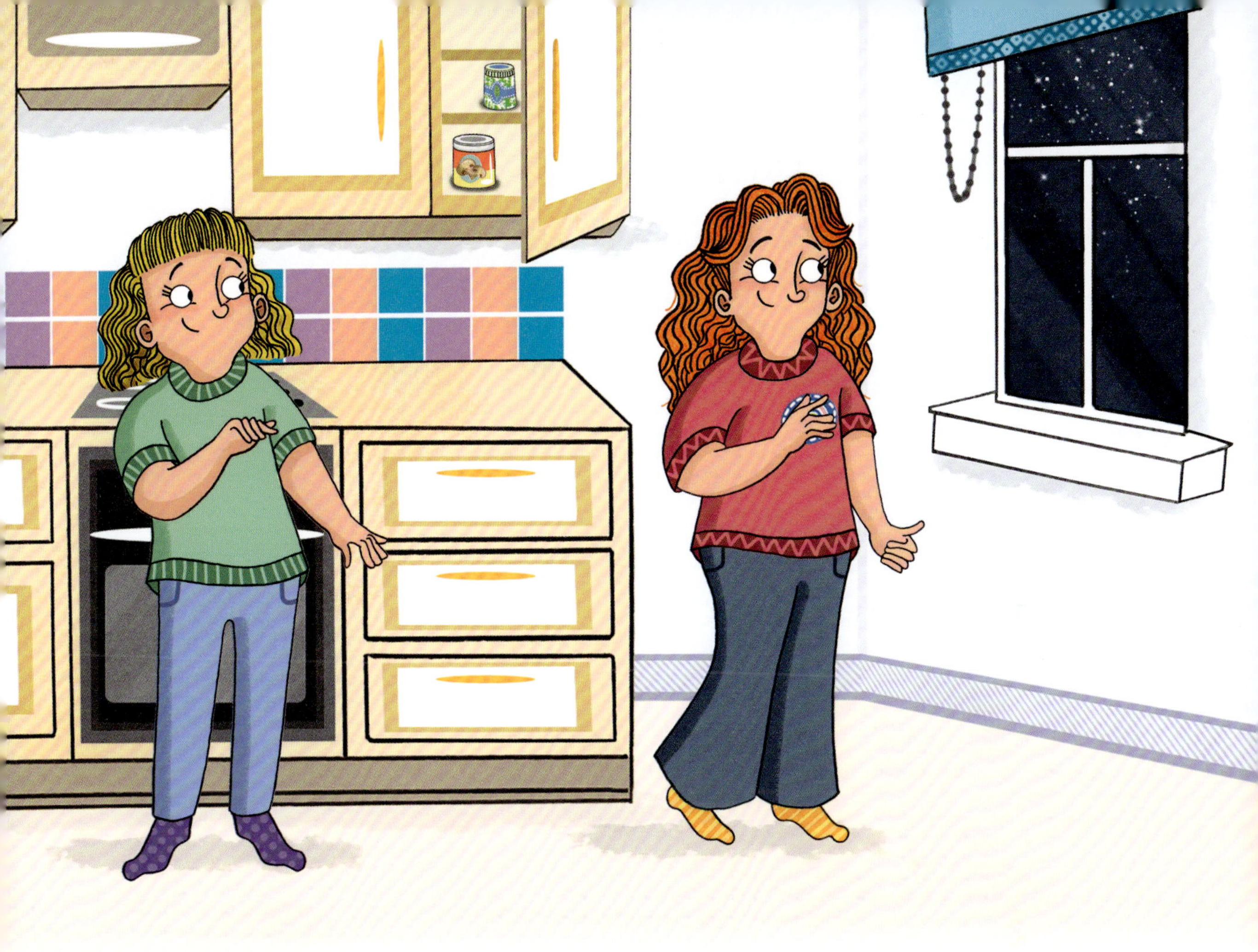

The rest of the kitchen was mostly empty, too.

"Shall we eat out?" Sasha suggested.

"Yes!" Jane cried. "Let's have a starlit picnic."

Sasha smiled. That wasn't what she meant, but it sounded fun.

"All finished," Lorraine cried. She reappeared with the most incredible jacket Sasha had ever seen.

"Thank you!" Sasha said, gratefully.

“Now let’s cook,” Jane said with a grin.

Sasha looked around, confused. “Cook what?”

Jane giggled. “A feast!”

She put together potatoes, mushroom soup, cheese and herbs. It smelled delicious.

They ate dinner in a nearby park.

"This is scrumptious!" Sasha cried, tucking in ravenously.

She beamed at Jane and Lorraine. Her heart was full. Who knew you could have so much fun without toys, TV or fancy food?

The next day, Sasha's mum gasped. "Where did you get that fabulous jacket?" she asked.

"Lorraine made it," Sasha beamed, twirling.

"Wow!" her mum cried. "Do you sell them?"

Lorraine chuckled. "I make them for fun. They're not good enough to sell," she said.

"Yes, they are, Mum!" Jane said.
"Everyone at school wants one," Sasha added.
"You're really talented," Sasha's mum agreed.
Lorraine blushed. "Thank you!" she said.

The following week, Jane rushed up to Sasha excitedly.

"Mum sold her first clothes!" she cried. "The orders are flooding in. Yesterday, we had cake as a special treat! It wasn't even my birthday."

Sasha beamed. "Congratulations!" she said.

Jane passed Sasha a box. "I've got a slice of cake for you. Without you, Mum would never have considered selling her clothes. We're so lucky you came for a sleepover," she said.

Sasha smiled, but shook her head. “I’m the lucky one, Jane. You’ve taught me so much,” Sasha said.

Jane beamed. “We’re both lucky to be such good friends,” she replied.

How to make your own one-of-a-kind clothes!

• Use fabric paint to add your own name or design.

• Add a pocket to cover a stain.

• Add sequins, ribbons, buttons or bows.

Ask students to read the instructions. Encourage them to talk about the types of clothes they might make.